PONTIUS' PUDDLE PRESENTS

THE PEACEABLE KINGDOM

and Other Fallacies of Faith

JOEL KAUFFMANN

Abingdon Press
Nashville

PONTIUS' PUDDLE PRESENTS
THE PEACEABLE KINGDOM AND OTHER FALLACIES OF FAITH

Copyright © 1997 by Abingdon Press

This book is printed on recycled, acid-free paper.

ISBN: 0-687-45919-2

The wolf also shall dwell with the lamb,
and the leopard shall lie down with the kid;
and the calf and the young lion and the fatling together;
then a totally boss bullfrog shall rule them.
—Isaiah 11:6 (Puddle Paraphrase)

The material in this book may be reproduced with permission by and payment to the artist. For more information contact:

JOEL KAUFFMANN
c/o ABINGDON PRESS
P.O. BOX 801
NASHVILLE, TN 37202-0801 USA

E-MAIL: PONTPUDL@AOL.COM

97 98 99 00 01 02 03 04 05 06 — 10 9 8 7 6 5 4 3 2 1

MANUFACTURED IN THE UNITED STATES OF AMERICA

CONTENTS

FOREWORD

What a fortunate choice of metaphor, *Pontius' Puddle*. A large frog in a small swamp resisting the temptation to pretend it a pond or claim it a lake. A bog, a log of his own, is enough of a bully pulpit to address issues of great—even global—moral, environmental, social, and spiritual import.

Pontius does not fail us. Confront us, affront us, surprise us, he is a constant nudge toward goals we fail to see or seek.

What shall we make of this irreverent frog?

Pontius is an inadvertent prophet. The only true kind. In his dismissal of others' views, his defaulting from responsibility for attitudes of his own, his irony cuts cleanly. He speaks truth. From his pulpit pad, he punctures pretensions, debunks duplicity, names our faults and foibles for what they are— sins of omission or commission.

Pontius is an unaware pundit. With his quick repartees which explode like eruptions of the unconscious, he speaks wisdom. His tuffet is his chair of applied philosophy. He has perfected the skill of instant formulation of timeless proverbs.

Pontius is also a reluctant poet. Poetry, the art of images, aesthetics, and insight in condensations is his second tongue, sometimes a forked tongue. He can frame a couplet with the best of frogs. His blank verse, at first glance doggerel, on second thought is haiku.

By the third strip of cartoons, readers will have recognized that his puddle is our puddle, his swamp is the morass of my struggling small group, your First Church on Main Street, or their megachurch by the freeway cloverleaf. We know Pontius because his world is the world we have made. His critiques are familiar lines mysteriously lifted from our uneasy consciences.

The amphibian is, by definition, capable of living in two worlds. Pontius does it well. Alter ego to a cartoonist aptly named for a stubborn prophet, he delivers the wit of Joel Kauffmann with the bite of honesty, the nip of revelation, the tug of compassion.

David Augsburger
Claremont, California

5

MY WORLD AND WELCOME TO IT!

Welcome to Pontius' Puddle, a small, shallow, sludge-filled wallow that just so happens to be in the exact center of the entire known universe.

For the creatures who reside here, this isolated pool was a carefree refuge until we began to recognize that the world beyond our boundaries was filled with need. No longer able to ignore the problems that surrounded us, we knew what we had to do: discipline ourselves not to care. So our creed became: *If it doesn't happen to me, how important can it be?* Maintaining a strong sense of apathy is no easy matter, particularly when God has perfected the art of inspiring guilt. As Chief Pontificator of the puddle, it became my job to reinterpret those nagging portions of Scripture that interfere with such time-honored pursuits as sunning on a rock or wallowing in the mud.

On the following pages, I share with you some of these insights. Study well and whenever you have the urge to fall asleep in church, pass a volunteer sheet along unsigned, toss a charity request into the trash, or surf past shots of hungry children on TV, rest assured my sentiments will be with you.

After all, why was the earth created three-quarters water if God didn't expect us to wash our hands of responsibility?

—Pontius

THE PEACEABLE KINGDOM

This notion is, of course, complete pond moss.

As it turned out, the Peaceable Kingdom William Penn sought to establish in the New World as a haven for those suffering religious persecution lasted only a short time. And its main contribution, I suspect, was to lull Native Americans into a false sense of complacency so that those who followed in Willie's well-meaning wake could more easily steal their land.

The Bible makes no actual reference to a Peaceable Kingdom, more realistically predicting that there will always be wars and rumors of wars. And without wars, think where we'd be. War is responsible for much of our population control and advances in technology, not to mention some of our coolest movies and most interesting segments on the nightly news.

Sure, Scripture does suggest that the lamb will lie down with the lion. What it fails to mention is that moments later, the woolly creature would be nuttin' but mutton.

2 *God*
Spiritual Life
Scripture
Sin

IN GOD WE TRUST

I won't quarrel with this—particularly with the Supreme Wielder of Lightning Bolts standing watch overhead. I will suggest, however, that even a casual check of we creatures' commitments clearly shows God to be pretty far down on the list of things in which we put our faith, following such items as:

Money
Military Might
Medicine
Litigation
Politics
Private Education
Science
Sex
Sports
Retirement Funds
Public Education
That Lucky Penny in Our Loafers

The odd thing is, in spite of this, God continues to trust us to exercise domain over all creation. In my view, then, God has only himself to blame for the total mess we've made of things.

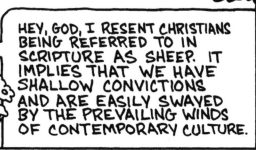

17

Panel 1: PONTIUS, SPEAK TO US ON THE NATURE OF SIN...

I PREFER TO LET MY ACTIONS SPEAK FOR THEMSELVES.

Panel 2: HOW SHOULD A CHRISTIAN VIEW SIN?

PREFERABLY FROM A GREAT DISTANCE!

Panel 3: HOW DOES THE CLERGY VIEW SIN?

AS JOB SECURITY!

Panel 4: WHAT IS THE WORST SIN OF ALL?

SOMEONE ELSE'S.

Panel 5: WHO SAID "MAN'S NATURE IS SINFUL"?

IT MUST HAVE BEEN A WOMAN.

Panel 6: DID SIN BEGIN WITH THE APPLE?

NO, BUT THE COMPUTER IS HELPING US TO SIN MORE EFFICIENTLY.

Panel 7: HOW CAN ONE SIN LESS?

TAKE LOTS OF NAPS!

Panel 8: MUST WE FORGIVE 70 TIMES 7?

I KNOW A LAWYER WHO CAN GET YOU 17 TIMES 7.

20

3 *Poverty*
Hunger
Homelessness
Christian Service

I WAS HUNGRY AND YOU FED ME

ike we really have a choice. In Matthew 25, God makes it abundantly clear that those who fail to follow this simple directive will be cast into the fiery pits of hell. A good lawyer could make the case that God is talking only to sheep and goats. But assuming other creatures, including amphibians, are being addressed, I for one am not taking any chances.

Speaking for the affluent, however, I feel we have earned the right to help define the "least of these" whom we're being coerced to help.

Certainly it should not include able-bodied adults. Any who find themselves hungry for fault of their own—such as living in an area of the world afflicted by drought or war—should pack up their bags and move to a better neighborhood.

I was going to argue that we shouldn't have to feed creatures in countries we consider enemies, but since we're now learning that most of the food we consume causes cancer, heart problems, or some other malady, I now say: feed 'em first!

24

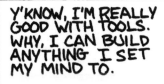

THOSE WILLING TO THEOLOGIZE ABOUT, EXPOUND UPON, ANALYZE, FORM COMMITTEES TO STUDY, ADMINISTER, FACILITATE, AND CONTRIBUTE MONEY TOWARDS THE WORK OF THE CHURCH.

THOSE WILLING TO DO THE WORK OF THE CHURCH.

TODAY'S CHURCH HAS GROWN IRRELEVANT, IMPERVIOUS TO THE NEEDS OF THE WORLD.

PREACH IT, BROTHER.

SOMEONE MUST PAY FOR THIS APATHY!

DON'T GO TOO HARD ON YOURSELF.

ME?

CERTAINLY. THE CHURCH IS SIMPLY THE SUM TOTAL OF ITS MEMBERS.

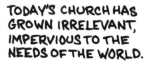

YIKES! I HAVE MET THE APATHY AND IT IS I.

4 Worship Sermons Community Sacraments

I WAS GLAD WHEN THEY SAID UNTO ME; LET US GO INTO THE HOUSE OF THE LORD

Oh really? I just conducted a survey at my congregation and the figures I came up with were:

40 percent annoyed
30 percent apathetic
20 percent grumpy

Of those interviewed, only 10 percent responded *glad*, and it happened to be raining hard at the time. Furthermore, once inside the house of the Lord, almost all agreed that they immediately became quite lethargic.

One humble suggestion: If we really want to make our church buildings the House of the Lord, maybe we should take a few cues from our own homes. I mean, how would your guests feel if you invited them over, coerced them to wear their funeral duds, sit for long stretches on really uncomfortable furniture, and look at the back of the others' heads while someone else did all the talking?

THE PASTOR'S SERMONS ARE LOUSY. THE SONGLEADER IS SLUGGISH. OUR SUNDAY SCHOOL TEACHERS ARE AS DULL AS POND SLUDGE. AND, THE YOUTH MINISTER IS TOO OFF-THE-WALL!

ALL MEMBERS ARE GIVEN A GIFT. MINE HAPPENS TO BE POINTING OUT WHAT'S WRONG WITH EVERYBODY ELSE'S!

THOSE WISHING TO ATTEND A RETREAT ON PROCLAIMING FAITH IN A SECULAR AGE, PLEASE SEE ME AFTER THE SERVICE.

NEXT WEEKEND, THE YOUTH WILL BE HAVING A RETREAT ON SEX AND DRUGS, UH, HOW TO AVOID THEM, THAT IS.

OUR WOMEN'S RETREAT THIS YEAR WILL FOCUS ON FAMILIES IN CRISIS.

NO WONDER THE CHURCH HAS TROUBLE MAKING PROGRESS. EVERY TIME WE HAVE A PROBLEM, WE "RETREAT."

YOU KNOW IT'S BEEN TOO LONG SINCE YOU LAST ATTENDED CHURCH WHEN:

• They've undergone a building program, and you aren't able to find the sanctuary.

• The greeters at the door ask you to sign the guest registry.

• That bratty kid who used to bug you is now head usher.

• You head for your favorite pew, but can't remember where it's located.

• You have to fake the Lord's Prayer.

• You're shocked to learn that King James is no longer the only Bible translation.

• You hear the same sermon as last time, and the pastor preaches on a 7-year cycle.

• The last time you put a quarter in the offering plate, it really was a tenth of your income.

• That guy who shows up just for Easter shoots you a sanctimonious look.

R-R-RING!

HI, IT'S PONTIUS. I JUST HAD THAT HORRIBLE NIGHTMARE AGAIN.

PONTIUS, BELIEVE ME, IT'S HIGHLY IMPROBABLE THAT YOU'LL BE ABDUCTED AND FORCED TO JOIN A LITURGICAL DANCE GROUP. NOW, GO BACK TO SLEEP.

I'LL TRY.

WHY DOES THE LEADER MAKE US SING EVERY VERSE?

50 MINUTES! THE PASTOR JUST SET A NEW RECORD FOR SERMONS.

OH NO! NOT A SHARING TIME.

IF I WASN'T SUCH A SINNER, I'D SKIP CHURCH ALTOGETHER!

SIGH, IF YOU CAN'T DO THE TIME, DON'T DO THE CRIME!!!

5. Children
Youth
Sunday School
Nurture

THE INNOCENCE OF CHILDREN

I can't say what kids were like in first-century Galilee. But I suspect Jesus might have had second thoughts about telling his followers that they must become like children to enter the kingdom of God had he observed the modern generation weaned on television and video games.

With these gadgets, the average tyke witnesses about seven thousand acts of simulated violence per year on TV and commits about ten times that many playing video games. If we adults acted like that in real life, a lot of creatures would be headed to Kingdom Come a whole lot quicker.

Fortunately, most of us have heeded the command in 1 Corinthians 13:11 to put away childish things and behave like grownups (the notable exception being at church business meetings).

As we age, unfortunately, we all succumb to the second childhood where, at the first sign of senility, these "innocent" kids ship us off to institutions and swaddle us in Depends. Which is why we frogs take the opportunity, while our offspring are still in the tadpole stage, to eat as many of them as we can.

39

MY SUNDAY SCHOOL TEACHER JUST HANDED OUT YEAR-END EVALUATIONS.

HOW'D YOU DO?

"PONTIUS FAILED TO READ THE ASSIGNMENTS, SLEPT DURING INPUT, AND DERAILED DISCUSSION WITH ADDLE-BRAINED OPINIONS."

FLUNKED, HUH?

ACTUALLY, I WAS NAMED MOST VALUABLE MEMBER.

FOR WHAT?

I BRING GREAT SNACKS!

CARE TO JOIN MY CLASS?

HURRY UP, PONTIUS. WE GOT A SUNDAY SCHOOL PARTY, A YOUTH GROUP SERVICE PROJECT, AND A YOUNG ADULT BIBLE STUDY ALL WAITING FOR PIZZA.

PIZZA

FAITH MAY MOVE MOUNTAINS, BUT IT ALSO MOVES A LOT OF MOZZARELLA!

PIZZA

44

THE SANCTITY OF LIFE

In today's world, this is a touchy topic. So allow me to display my sensitivity to the prevailing sentiment by waxing poetic:

> Roses are red.
> Violets are blue.
> God made me sacred.
> Too bad about you!

About the only thing it seems we can all agree on is the sanctity of our own life. After that it starts getting tricky.

Taking another's life in self-defense is certainly all right, because it was either them or me.

We believe in reconciliation, but if we don't fry a few murderers now and then, our society will disintegrate into total chaos.

According to science, a fetus may or may not be a complete human being, but even if it is, how dare it inconvenience the control I exercise over my own body.

In war, of course, killing is not only acceptable, it is honorable, and all the more so if the enemy is trying to deprive me of my divine right to petroleum.

I end with another poem:

> Violets are blue.
> Roses are red.
> When we justify killing,
> The truth winds up dead!

45

THE GIFT OF LIFE

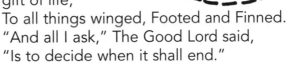

A Poem by Pontius

God
breathed
out the
gift of life,
To all things winged, Footed and Finned.
"And all I ask," The Good Lord said,
"Is to decide when it shall end."

"Certainly!" The grateful creatures cried,
"Our judgment we will hold,
Unless confronted by a fetus unwanted,
or an invalid grown too old.

"Of course if order is to be maintained,
We'll need the death penalty,
But other than that you have our word . . .
Uh, we did mention war, didn't we?"

"What have I wrought?" God sighed,
With considerable chagrin.
"Maybe instead of breathing out
The time has come to breathe in."

GRACE VS. WORKS

EVOLUTION VS. CREATION

CHIMP

USE OF STYROFOAM CUPS AT CHURCH PICNICS

GREAT RELIGIOUS DEBATES IN HISTORY

THE IDEA OF EVOLUTION IS RIDICULOUS! HOW CAN ANYONE THINK THAT MAN EVOLVED FROM A BRUTAL BEAST ENSLAVED BY HIS OWN PRIMITIVE PASSIONS TO BECOME A CREATURE OF WISDOM AND CULTURE?

YOU'RE RIGHT. BUT DON'T GIVE UP HOPE. GIVEN ENOUGH TIME, IT STILL COULD HAPPEN!

HEY, WAIT A MINUTE. BURP

HERE, HAVE A BANANA.

UMM. BANANA GOOD!

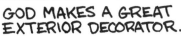

UNTO THE UTTERMOST PART OF THE EARTH

I'm a firm believer in a literal interpretation of the Bible . . . particularly when it suits my purposes. For those who, like myself, live in constant fear of having to put their faith into actual words, let me put you at ease by reexamining Acts 1:8, where we are instructed to witness in Jerusalem, Judea, and unto the uttermost part of the earth.

It is, of course, illegal to witness in Jerusalem today. And ancient Judea can no longer be found in the atlas.

That leaves the uttermost part of the earth, which according to my dictionary, means the farthest or most extreme point.

Checking the opposite side of the globe, the farthest point for me falls way out in the ocean. While fish may serve as a fine symbol for Christianity, in my experience they make far better filets than converts.

Having disposed of the need to witness with words, I turn to a more troublesome hypothesis: that we also witness with our deeds. Perhaps you find the following illustration as disturbing as do I: *An evangelist passing through the countryside encountered a farmer and proceeded to ask the humble man if he was saved. "I could tell you anything," replied the farmer. "If you really want to know, then ask my neighbors."*

TV EVANGELIST SERIES

WHEREVER TWO OR THREE ARE GATHERED TOGETHER...

...SOMEBODY REALLY OUGHT TO START A MEMBERSHIP DRIVE!!!

SIGH. ONCE UPON A TIME, OUR CHURCH'S MISSION PROGRAMS WERE MOSTLY OVERSEAS. NOW THEY'RE MOSTLY OVERLOOKED.

FOLLOW THE LEADER

The Native Americans had a great concept for leadership. The tribal chief would pack up his tepee and move to another location. If the tribe chose to follow, his leadership was affirmed.

This, unfortunately, would not work well with my congregation. First of all, we own the parsonage and prefer not to chase it down. Second, for some odd reason, the last five pastors who departed have refused to leave any forwarding address.

We're currently trying to assess why we have such a rapid turnover in leadership. Certainly it's not the pastoral search team. After meeting continually for the past fifteen years, we've become closely bonded. And, the job description we've formed for our prospective pastors is positively God-like: *"To work endless hours and be everywhere at once."*

We want our next pastor to call the congregation to a deeper level of discipleship and piety. We also insist that the pastor have a strong sense of grace . . . which certainly will be needed when we promptly proceed to ignore that call.

61

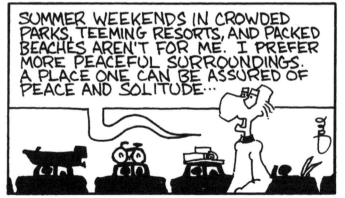

63

SILVER AND GOLD HAVE I NONE

. . . because my dough is all tied up in stock options and treasury bonds. Of all the fallacies of faith, the notion that we should renounce wealth wins the gold medal hands down.

Sure, Jesus poked fun at the rich and praised the poor. Then again, that may have just been sour grapes from a guy who had the hard luck of being a carpenter in a land that has only two trees and ten zillion stones.

Two thousand years later, we've become much more enlightened and now recognize wealth as a virtue, not a vice. When confronted by an empty-pocketed prophet, we're quick to retort: "If you're so religious, why aren't you rich?"

You disagree? Try counting how many itinerant carpenters currently serve on churchwide committees and boards. In fact, about the only time our ecclesiastical leaders talk against money is when they're trying to separate us from ours. Did you know that the original Greek word for stewardship, *oikonomia*, actually means "watch your wallet"? When asked to give till it hurts, I now place my money in a back pocket where I can't reach it without activating an old tennis injury.

In conclusion, we must diligently resist those who would revise the sage of Job by suggesting:

> *The Devil is much wiser*
> *Than in days of yore,*
> *And tempts by making rich*
> *Instead of making poor.*

PLUNK

WOW, A QUARTER! THANKS TO YOU, PONTIUS, THE FIGHT AGAINST EVIL CAN CONTINUE!!!

THINGS HAVE EITHER GOTTEN TOUGHER THAN I THOUGHT, OR GOD HAS TAKEN UP SARCASM.

DO YOU REALIZE THAT CHRISTIANS NUMBER ONLY 32% OF THE WORLD'S POPULATION, YET THEY RECEIVE 62% OF THE ENTIRE WORLD'S INCOME. AND THEY SPEND 97% OF IT ON THEMSELVES!

LET'S SEE YOU LAUGH THAT STATISTIC AWAY WITH SOME STUPID WISECRACK...WELL GO AHEAD. I'M WAITING.

WORKING IN A RELIGIOUS CARTOON STRIP CAN HAVE ITS TOUGHER MOMENTS.

69

10

Stress
Holistic Health
Lifestyle

OUR BODIES ARE GOD'S TEMPLE

Most people, upon hearing this statement, assume that we should honor God's presence within us by staying fit. Nothing could be farther from the truth. During Jesus' time on earth, he may have visited a spiffy temple or two, but he clocked a lot more time mixing it up in some pretty squalid surroundings.

And, Jesus did his share of eating and drinking. His first miracle was to create a beverage, and one of his last acts was to throw a feast for his disciples. It's a shame, I maintain, that at communion time, we memorialize this festive supper with a stingy square of bread and scant swallow of juice.

I say, then, that if our bodies are truly God's temple, let's put those donuts and chocolate bars God bestowed upon us to good use and give the Almighty a lot more room in which to work.

Having said that, I do try to take my doctor's advice seriously. She suggested I lower my cholesterol level when I eat, so I sawed off the legs of my dining chairs. She also advised that I develop a Master plan for my spiritual, mental, and physical health, which I did: I'm waiting for sloth, stress, and flab to come back in style.

WELCOME, CLASS. ONCE AGAIN OUR TOPIC IS **OVEREATING.** TWO WEEKS AGO WE DECIDED THERE ARE WORSE VICES A CREATURE COULD HAVE, AND LAST WEEK WE...

CONCLUDED THAT STARVING PEOPLE WOULDN'T GET OUR LEFTOVERS ANYWAY. TODAY WE'LL EXAMINE THE BENEFIT TO THE FARMER...

RATIONALIZATION 101 IS A POPULAR COURSE !!!

YOU HAVE TO THINK OF JOGGING AS A SPIRITUAL EXPERIENCE.

HUFF, PUFF, I DO-- PERSECUTION!

JUST SET YOUR MIND IN AN ATTITUDE OF **PRAISE.**

THAT'S, GASP, NOT SO EASY WHEN YOUR BODY IS IN A STATE OF **PETITION!**

ANIMAL

MINERAL

VEGETABLE

THE CHURCH IS CALLING A WEEKEND RETREAT FOR COUPLES ON MARRIAGE COMMITMENTS.

WHO NEEDS IT, HUH?

YEAH, MOST OF US HAVE BEEN RETREATING FROM OUR COMMITMENTS SINCE THE HONEYMOON ENDED!

MY JOB WAS CREATING TOO MUCH STRESS IN MY LIFE. SO, I BEGAN DAILY DEVOTIONS, EXERCISING REGULARLY, AND SPENDING QUALITY TIME WITH FRIENDS AND FAMILY.

SO... DO YOU FEEL LESS STRESS FROM YOUR JOB?

MUCH! TO DO ALL THOSE THINGS, I HAD TO GIVE IT UP!

WE CREATURES HAVE COME A LONG WAY SINCE WE WORSHIPPED THE GOLDEN CALF!

NOW WE WORSHIP BOTH CALVES, OUR THIGHS, BICEPS, NOT TO MENTION THE ABDOMEN.

WE ARE ALL CREATED EQUAL IN CHRIST

Red, brown, yellow, black, and white are all equal in God's sight, and just a notch below green.

Yes, I'm prejudiced and proud of it. As I see it, if God didn't mean for us to be a little prejudiced, why bother to make us different?

Humans spend a lot of energy and create a lot of unnecessary stress claiming to subscribe to a rainbow coalition, while at the same time segregating every aspect of their life not covered by a court order.

We in the animal kingdom have a distinct advantage. Our differences are directly linked to our dining habits. Perhaps in heaven, wolves and lambs, leopards and goats, bovines and bears, bullfrogs and bald eagles will pose together for portraits, but here on earth, such a scenario would be nothing more than a setup for a feeding frenzy.

Panel 1: I HAVE A DREAM-- WHERE CREATURES ARE NO LONGER DIVIDED JUST BY THE COLOR OF THEIR SKIN, BUT BY CLASS AND IDEOLOGY. WHERE THE RICH THIRD OF THE WORLD...

Panel 2: ...CONTINUES TO ACCUMULATE WEALTH, WHILE THE POOREST TWO-THIRDS ARE CONDEMNED TO LIVES OF INCREASING SQUALOR.

Panel 3: NOT VERY INSPIRING, BUT YOU'VE GOT TO ADMIT, IT HAS AN AIR OF AUTHENTICITY.

IT'S NOT EASY BEING GREEN!

BECAUSE WE LIVE IN A WORLD FULL OF PREJUDICE WHERE ONE IS JUDGED BY THE COLOR OF ONE'S SKIN?

NO, BECAUSE WE APPEAR IN A PUBLICATION THAT IS PRINTED IN BLACK AND WHITE!

12 *Politics*
Influence of Media
Church History

THE SEPARATION OF CHURCH AND STATE

In my opinion, this is an idea whose time has come . . . and gone. Here, then, I pontificate my reasons why we should bring back the ancient idea of Christendom, or a reunited alliance between the Church and State:

1. First of all, how bad can an idea be that lasted almost twelve centuries (circa the fourth to the sixteenth)? In my congregation, we can't stick with anything for twelve weeks!

2. With only one religion, we could completely eliminate interfaith wars.

3. Since, under Christendom, all members of society would automatically belong to the church, we would also save a bundle on missions.

4. With TV talk shows running out of topics, heretics could be a cool new category for guest material (or hot, depending on their method of execution).

5. Since the church was created for sinners, our clergy would have more direct access to the acknowledged champions of deceit and depravity: politicians.

So my vote for Christendom is cast, providing the hierarchy meet one small demand: that when the mandated doctrine is formed, I get the first right of approval!

Panel 1: FORTUNATELY, FOR THOSE OF US WHO UNDERSTAND THAT A MORALLY AMBIGUOUS SOCIETY NEEDS HEROES-- ONE'S BORN EVERY MINUTE.

A HERO?

Panel 2: NO-- A SUCKER!

WHY DO THEY GIVE THESE FILMS TWO-SYLLABLE TITLES?

SO THEIR TARGET AUDIENCE IS ABLE TO READ THEM.

NOW SHOWING
I ROCKY
II RAMBO
III COBRA

Panel 3: PEOPLE ACCUSE WE MEDIA MOGULS OF NOT BEING CREATIVE.

Panel 4: BAL-DER-DASH!

Panel 5: WHO ELSE COULD PERSUADE THE PUBLIC THAT ENDLESS HOURS OF EXPOSURE TO GRATUITOUS VIOLENCE HAVE NO IMPACT ON OUR VIEWERS...

Panel 6: WHILE CONTINUING TO CONVINCE OUR COMMERCIAL SPONSORS THAT THEIR THIRTY SECOND SPOTS DO!

NEW

IN THE BEGINNING WAS THE WORD... FOR CENTURIES SCRIPTURE WAS PRESERVED ON TABLETS AND SCROLLS. MASS-PRINTED MANUSCRIPTS FINALLY MADE THE BIBLE AVAILABLE TO ALL.

WITH THE ADVENT OF RADIO AND TV, THE GOSPEL TOOK TO THE AIR. AND NOW COMPUTERS OFFER THE CHURCH A CHANCE TO GO ON-LINE. CAST OUR NET OUT OVER THE INTERNET. WITNESS VIA THE WEB. EVANGELIZE BY E-MAIL!

JUST ONE MORE GAME OF MINESWEEPER AND I KNOW I CAN BREAK TWO-HUNDRED.

SHALL I KEEP STALLING THE NEW MEMBERS CLASS?

MENTION THAT NEW MARKET-DRIVEN MEGA-CHURCH THAT JUST OPENED ACROSS TOWN!

NOAH, WE'VE GOT A PROBLEM!

THE REAL REASON DINOSAURS BECAME EXTINCT

13

Thanksgiving
Christmas
New Year
Valentine's Day
Easter

THE JOY OF THE HOLIDAYS

As I see it, joy during the holidays is a relative thing: the more relatives who show up, the less I enjoy it. Instead of decking the halls, we soon feel like decking one another.

Perhaps we went wrong when we began to expect that our holidays should be filled with joy.

I think our medieval forebears had it right. Back then, suffering was the object of religious holidays, not merely a by-product. On such occasions,

THE NEXT TIME I ANSWER A JOB DESCRIPTION FOR SOMETHING FAT AND GREEN, I'M GOING TO READ THE FINE PRINT FIRST!

penitent pilgrims dressed themselves in rough sackcloth and set out barefoot over rocky roads to pay homage to their holy shrines.

We do have one thing to celebrate. During medieval times there were dozens of religious holidays. Today, we've man-

aged to minimize our misery by drastically reducing that number.

At this point in history, we're probably stuck with the festivities of Thanksgiving and Christmas, but perhaps we could find a portion of peace if we downplayed the euphoria of Easter and focused more on the solemnity of Good Friday instead.

91

THUMB THUMB

GOT A PROBLEM?

YEAH.

THUMB

I CAN NEVER REMEMBER IF THE THANKSGIVING STORY IS IN THE OLD OR NEW TESTAMENT.

HE ROSE FROM HUMBLE BEGINNINGS TO BECOME KING. HE PROVIDED HOPE AND INSPIRATION TO MILLIONS. SNIFF, THOSE OF US WHO TRULY BELIEVE HE LIVES ON CONTINUE TO MAKE PILGRIMAGES TO WHERE IT ALL BEGAN.

CHRIST'S MANGER IN BETHLEHEM?

NO, ELVIS' MANSION AT GRACELAND!

SIGH. IF THE END TIMES AREN'T NEAR, THEY SHOULD BE.

I TOLD OUR CHILDREN'S CLASS THE CHRISTMAS STORY-- HOW THE WISE MEN WERE LED BY A STAR, AND HOW THE SHEPHERDS SAW THE SKY FILL WITH LIGHT AND HEARD THE VOICES OF ANGELS.

HOW'D THE KIDS RESPOND?

THEY WANTED TO KNOW WHO CREATED THE SPECIAL EFFECTS.

WELL, PONTIUS, WHAT DO YOU THINK?

DO YOU REALIZE THAT 20 MILLION PEOPLE DIED OF HUNGER THIS PAST YEAR? THAT'S 200 TIMES MORE THAN THE NUMBER OF NEEDLES ON THIS TREE.

PROPHETS ARE NOT APPRECIATED IN THEIR OWN LAND... NOR DURING THE HOLIDAY SEASON.

ZIKES! WHAT A YEAR. JOSEPH FORGOT TO MAKE RESERVATIONS AT THE BETHLEHEM INN (HIS CARPENTRY PRODUCTS AREN'T THE ONLY OBJECTS MADE OUT OF WOOD). SO THEY STICK US IN THIS STABLE FULL OF STALE HAY AND STINKING ANIMALS AND GUESS WHAT? I GO RIGHT INTO LABOR. "NO PROBLEM," MY OBSTETRICIAN SAID, "MAKE THE TRIP." ANYWAY, WE HAVE A NEW BABY BOY THAT WE THINK IS TRULY SPECIAL, BUT IT'S BEEN A MADHOUSE EVER SINCE. FIRST, WE CAN'T AGREE ON A NAME. JOSEPH LIKES IMMANUEL; I'M HOLDING OUT FOR JESUS!

NEXT, ALL THESE SHEPHERDS STOP BY TO GAWK (AS IF THE SMELL WASN'T BAD ENOUGH). AT LEAST THOSE THREE CAMEL JOCKEYS BROUGHT GIFTS (EVER TRY TO EXCHANGE MYRRH WITHOUT A RECEIPT?). WE CAN'T GET A GOOD NIGHT'S SLEEP WITH THAT STUPID STAR SHINING THROUGH THE CRACKS IN THE CEILING, AND EVERY STORE IN TOWN IS SOLD OUT OF SWADDLING. WELL, GOT TO GO. JOSEPH HAD ANOTHER GOOFY VISION, SO I GUESS WE'RE OFF TO EGYPT. THIS TIME, I MAKE THE RESERVATIONS. ALL MY LOVE, Mary

THE FIRST CHRISTMAS LETTER

NOW'S OUR CHANCE TO SATIRIZE THE GREED AND COMMERCIALIZATION OF CHRISTMAS. JUST SAY WHAT'S ON YOUR MIND.

PEACE ON EARTH AND GOD'S RICHEST BLESSING TO YOU AND YOURS.

I HOPE YOU REALIZE YOU JUST BLEW A PERFECTLY GOOD CARTOON STRIP.

ON THE GARDEN GOD LOOKED DOWN
AND SAID THAT "IT IS SWEET,"
BUT SOMETHING MORE IS NEEDED
FOR MY WORLD TO BE COMPLETE.

SO MALE AND FEMALE GOD CREATED,
INFUSED US WITH ROMANTIC BLISS,
AND WE MATED-- PROCREATED,
BUT ALAS THINGS WENT AMISS!

FOR WE ALSO FOUGHT AND ARGUED
ALONG OUR MATRIMONIAL COURSE.
AND MANY A COUPLING ENDED
IN THE BITTERNESS OF DIVORCE.

STILL, WE HONOR GOD'S BEQUEST
WITH AN ANNUAL HOLIDAY.
WE SEND OUT FRILLY VALENTINES
AND CONCOCT SWEET THINGS TO SAY.

YET WE WONDER IF THE CELEBRATION OF
THIS LOVE WITH WHICH WE'RE CURSED...

... OUGHT NOT BE MOVED
FROM FEBRUARY 14,
AND REASSIGNED
TO APRIL FIRST!

AS WE LOOK AHEAD TO EASTER, WE ARE REMINDED THAT WHAT WE GAINED SO JOYFULLY AT CHRISTMAS, WE MUST NOW LOSE WITH SUFFERING AND ANGUISH.

YOU MEAN OUR SAVIOR BORN IN BETHLEHEM?

NO, OUR EXTRA POUNDS FROM PIGGING OUT!

14. Heaven
Hell
Judgment Day

STREETS OF GOLD

In Revelation 21, the streets of New Jerusalem, or heaven, are described as being paved with pure gold. I won't quarrel with Scripture; I simply suggest that this is a clear case of poetic license.

If heaven were really girded with golden boulevards, it seems to me you'd see a lot more people getting out of investment banking and into road construction.

Furthermore, God wouldn't play such a cruel prank. Why coat the landscape with cold currency when everything you could desire is free for all of eternity?

Assuming Saint John the Divine conjured up golden streets as a positive image to lure patrons onto the straight and narrow, then such descriptions must be altered when adapting the Bible for other cultures. In my own amphibian translation, for instance, heaven is described as a scummy pond swarming with an infestation of fat flies. Hell, on the other hand, is viewed as a formaldehyde-filled specimen jar in a biology lab.

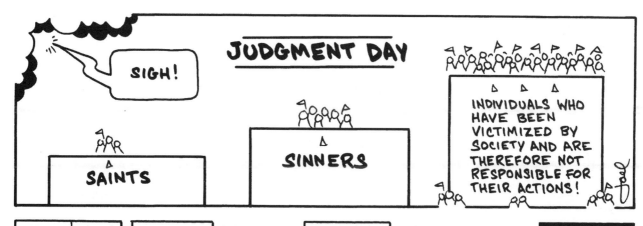

IT'S GREAT TO KNOW THAT IF YOU LOVE GOD, YOU GO TO HEAVEN WHEN YOU DIE.

IMAGINE WORRYING IF YOU'LL WIND UP IN HELL, OR COME BACK AS A TSE TSE FLY, OR THAT IT'S ALL OVER AFTER YOU EXPIRE.

WITHOUT FAITH, I GUESS THE AFTERLIFE IS JUST LIKE A BOX OF CHOCOLATES-- YOU NEVER KNOW WHAT YOU'RE GOING TO GET!

SO YOU SEE, PONTIUS, GOD DOESN'T CARE HOW SMART ONE IS, BUT WHETHER ONE HAS A PERSONAL RELATIONSHIP WITH HIM.

HOW ABOUT THAT. EVEN ON JUDGMENT DAY IT WON'T BE HOW MUCH YOU KNOW THAT COUNTS -- BUT WHO YOU KNOW.

PERMISSION TO COPY

Persons reproducing the copyrighted cartoons from this book without permission may or may not be sued in a court of law, but they will be inflicted with a case of unsightly warts (or so the toad whom Pontius has retained as his lawyer warns).

Those God-fearing individuals wishing to do the right thing can get warm approval to reproduce a cartoon in their publication, or receive a monthly packet of *Pontius' Puddle* strips (the packet is free and subscribers pay for only those cartoons they use), by simply contacting:

Joel Kauffmann
c/o Abingdon Press
P.O. Box 801
Nashville, TN 37202-0801 USA

E-mail: PONTPUDL@AOL.COM